D1102440

FROGS
IN CREAM

FROGS
IN CREAM

Sparkling resources for speakers

Stephen Gaukroger and Nick Mercer

Scripture Union
130 City Road, London EC1V 2NJ

First published by Scripture Union, 1990.
130 City Road, London EC1V 2NJ.

British Library Cataloguing in Publication Data
 Gaukroger, Stephen 1954–
 Frogs in cream: sparkling resources
 for speakers.
 I. Title II. Mercer, Nick
 828.91402

 ISBN 0 86201 714 9

Cartoons by Taffy.

Phototypeset by Input Typesetting Ltd, London.
Printed and bound in Great Britain by Cox &
Wyman Ltd, Reading.

Contents

Dedication

Dedicated to Spurgeon's College, where learning
and laughter meet.

Acknowledgements

We are grateful to all those from whom we have
borrowed material for this collection – both
inadvertently and 'vertently'!

INTRODUCTION

This book is written in the hope that sermons, speeches and talks of every kind can be given a new lease of life. It arises from the belief that a good illustration reaches parts of a congregation that other homiletic techniques cannot reach.

This collection of illustrative material is offered to the planet in the hope of world-wide renewal, restoration and revival. Failing that, we'd settle for a lot fewer congregations and audiences being bored to death by worthy, yet dull, presentations. For too many listeners, the *Te Deum* has been replaced by *tedium*. The Good News deserves better!

+ Stephen Stopsley
+ Nicholas Northwood

THE ART

OF

ILLUSTRATION

1

Illustrations:
finding and using them

To most modern congregations, illustrations are like the ketchup on the burger, the cream on the strawberries or the chocolate flake in the ice-cream. You can exist without them but it's so much 'tastier' when they are there! Most speakers know the value of good illustrations – but where do you get them from? Well, you could:

● Develop your powers of observation. Daily life is a rich source of funny, sad and poignant incidents. Train yourself to look for them.

● Keep pen and paper handy. Write down possible illustrations as you come across them on TV, in the paper, in the shower or in general reading.

● Read biographies. People are interested in other people . . . particularly famous other people!

● 'Steal' them from other speakers!

● Use the little stories at the bottom of the page in the *Readers' Digest*.

● Subscribe to *Church News Service*, a magazine which will keep you supplied with features, quotes, ideas and illustrations. (*Church News Service*, 37B New Cavendish Street, London W1M 8JR.)

Illustrations usually need to 'illustrate' but occasionally they can be used effectively simply to give the congregation breathing space between the meatier sections of a sermon or talk. A short, illustrative 'mental break' is likely to increase the length of time the congregation or audience can concentrate.

Don't use too many illustrations, tell inappropriate jokes or pretend something happened to *you* when you got the story from a book! Timing is essential to watch, too: beware of giving the right illustration at the wrong time in the message. As a general rule, the nearer you get to the end of the talk, the less likely is humour to be appropriate.

Take up these suggestions, avoid the pitfalls, and then your illustrations won't be like ketchup on strawberries or chocolate flakes in your burgers!

2

Humour and the Bible

The Bible is a profoundly serious collection of writings yet it is also full of humour of every type, although this is sometimes lost in translation or through familiarity. A person with a good sense of humour almost always has good self-insight. Perhaps this is why so many of the Bible's writers used humour to comment incisively and memorably on issues of immense personal and national concern.

The Bible's humour ranges through:

● the *irony* of the Tower of Babel, built to reach 'up' to heaven – and God arranges an outing to go 'down' to see it (Genesis 11:4–5);

● the *pun* on Ehud, the left-handed Benjamite (Benjamin = 'son of my right hand'; Joshua 3:15);

● the 'lavatorial' *sarcasm* of Elijah on Carmel, mocking the no-show of the god Baal – 'perhaps he's on the loo?' (1 Kings 18:27);

● the *exaggeration* of Jesus – 'It's easier to get a camel through the eye of a needle than to get a rich person into heaven . . . !' (eg Luke 18:25);

- and even the *risqué innuendo* of Paul's barbed comment about some Jewish Christians who insisted that believers must be circumcised – 'If only the knife would slip . . . !' (Galatians 5:12).

If preaching is in part, 'truth through personality', then we, like the writers of the Bible, must use every aspect of our personality, including the gift of humour, to communicate God's truth.

3

Good and bad uses of humour

The Bible's humour is generally heavy on irony and light on sarcasm. Preachers down through the ages have sometimes taken the easy way out, though, and majored on sarcasm while ducking the harder work of irony. Even Luther and Calvin stooped to this. Spurgeon, too, the nineteenth-century prince of preachers who pulled in vast crowds, peppered his sermons with every form of wit – irony, pun, hyperbole, litotes, anecdote, parody, caricature, satire . . . and even a little sarcasm.

How can we use humour for the best advantage of our message, rather than to take advantage of others or of our position with a captive audience? Here are some suggestions of things to avoid and of ways to use humour.

Humour at its worst . . .

● is attention-seeking and reflects self-centredness.

● side-tracks a good raconteur by encouraging him to make the audience laugh even more!

19

- distracts an audience if used unthinkingly. A witticism may pop into the speaker's head, but speaking it out may destroy the atmosphere the Spirit was building.

- can be disastrous if accidental. For instance, a Spoonerism ('Who is a gardening pod like Thee . . . ') or a *double entendre* as a result of not being street-wise in the current use of language ('It was a gay evening . . . ') can cause the audience to roll around in hysterics while your serious message is lost for ever.

- is pastorally insensitive. Acts which leave people devastated, such as abortion, rape and child abuse, should never be referred to humorously. A wide range of others, including death, sex, homosexuality, feminism, politics and foreigners, can only be used with the utmost care and where you really know your audience.

- goes down like a pork pie in a synagogue if humour doesn't come naturally to you. If you're not comfortable using humour, neither will your congregation or audience be!

Humour at its best . . .

Use it:

● to illustrate the point.

● to gain a *rapport* with the audience, especially if they are unknown to you and to each other.

● to release unhelpful tension among the listeners, perhaps by defusing the pressure of a difficult subject, breaking up a long sermon or simply giving you and the audience time for a few deep breaths and a re-adjustment of clothes!

● to break through the listeners' defences, making them more open to what God has to say to them.

● to bring people down to earth, reminding us of humankind's foolishness and peeling away the pomposity and humbug with which we surround ourselves. Use humour to help us see our true, petty and paradoxical selves: full of noble aspirations and sordid fantasies – just like an impressive cathedral whose spire points us to heaven but whose gargoyles laugh down at us.

● to identify with our culture. Humour is one of the most powerful vehicles of communication in late twentieth-century western culture. People expect it, and it 'gets through' to them. Watch TV, listen to the radio, read the papers, popular magazines and books, and see how the advertisers use humour to 'sell' their wares.

● as one of God's greatest medicines for tired and

anxious minds. As Malcom Muggeridge, the former editor of *Punch* and late-in-life convert comments, 'Next to mystical enlightenment [laughter] is the most precious gift and blessing that comes to us on earth.'

THE A–Z

of stories, illustrations, anecdotes,

witticisms, etc . . .

Ageing

The seven ages of man: spills, drills, thrills, bills, ills, pills, wills. (Richard J Needham)

An anonymous prayer

Lord, thou knowest better than I know myself that I am growing older. Keep me from getting too talkative and thinking I must say something on every subject and on every occasion.

Release me from craving to straighten out everybody's affairs. Teach me the glorious lesson that, occasionally, it is possible that I may be mistaken.

Make me thoughtful, but not moody; helpful, but not bossy; for thou knowest, Lord, that I want a few friends at the end.

Little girl to old man with grey beard: 'Were you in the ark?'
'Goodness, no!'
Pause.
'Then why weren't you drowned?'

Someone is old if he or she is twenty years older than yourself.

Three signs of getting old:
1 Greying hair.
2 Memory loss.
And 3 . . . er . . . er . . .

Beatitudes for the aged

Blessed are they who understand
My faltering step and palsied hand.
Blessed are they who know my ears today
Must strain to catch the things they say.
Blessed are they who seem to know
My eyes are dim and wits are slow.
Blessed are they who look away
When coffee was spilt on the table today.
Blessed are they with a cheery smile,
Who stop to chat for a little while.
Blessed are they who never say,
'You've told that story twice today.'
Blessed are they who know the way
To bring back memories of yesterday.
Blessed are they who make it known
I'm loved, respected, and not alone.
Blessed are they who ease the days
On my journey home in loving ways.

*I'm sure he's not using that overhead
projector properly!*

Agnosticism

Did you hear about the agnostic, dyslexic, insomniac who lay awake at night wondering, 'Is there a Dog?'

Baptism

Church bulletin: On Tuesday afternoon there will be meetings in the north and south ends of the church. Children will be baptised at both ends.

Baptists

At a Baptist church meeting there was heated discussion about changing the church's name from Puddlington Baptist Church to Puddlington Christian Church.

Eventually, one old boy stood up and declared, 'I've been a Baptist for over fifty years and nobody's going to start calling *me* a Christian!'

How many Baptists does it take to change a light bulb?

A church meeting and about two-and-a-half years.

Bible

The Bible is so good, if it isn't true it ought to be!

A theologically liberal minister was visiting one of the elderly members of his congregation. He noticed that her Bible had hundreds of pages torn out of it, while many others had been cut up.

'What happened to your Bible?' he asked.

'Oh,' she replied, 'I just tear out all the bits you say we can't believe any more.'

No one ever graduates from Bible study until he meets its Author face to face. (Everett Harris)

The ten commandments

People nowadays treat the ten commandments like a history exam . . . they attempt only three.

David and Solomon lived right merry lives.
One had a thousand concubines, the other a
thousand wives.
But when, as they were growing old, they began
to have their qualms,
The one wrote the Proverbs and the other wrote
the Psalms.

Beatitudes for the twentieth century
(Matthew 5)

Blessed are the pushers, for they get on in the
world.
Blessed are the hard-boiled, for they never let life
hurt them.
Blessed are they who complain, for they get their
way in the end.
Blessed are the blasé, for they never worry over
their own sins.
Blessed are the slave-drivers, for they get results.
Blessed are the trouble-makers, for they make
people notice them.   (J B Phillips)

It's my new Swiss Army crozier!

31

Melody in F
(Luke 15: the story of the lost son)

Feeling footloose and frisky, a feather-brained
  fellow
Forced his fond father to fork over the farthings.
He flew far to foreign fields,
And frittered his fortune feasting fabulously with
  faithless friends.

Fleeced by his fellows in folly, and facing famine,
He found himself a feed-flinger in a filthy
  farmyard.
Fairly famishing, he fain would have filled his
  frame
With foraged food from fodder fragments.

'Fooey! My father's flunkies fare far finer!'
The frazzled fugitive forlornly fumbled, frankly
  facing facts.
Frustrated by failure, and filled with foreboding,
He fled forthwith to his family.

Falling at his father's feet, he forlornly fumbled,
'Father, I've flunked, and fruitlessly forfeited
  family fellowship favour.'
The far-sighted father, forestalling further
  flinching,
Frantically flagged the flunkies, 'Fetch a fatling
  from the flock and fix a feast!'

The fugitive's fault-finding brother frowned
On this fickle forgiveness of former falderal.

But the faithful father figured,
'Filial fidelity is fine, but the fugitive is found!
Let flags be unfurled! Let fanfares flare!'

His father's forgiveness formed the foundation
For the former fugitive's future fortitude.

John's Gospel

John's Gospel is 'like a magic pool where a child can paddle and an elephant can swim.' (Francis Moloney)

Acts

If you can't convince 'em with Matthew, Mark, Luke or John . . . hit 'em with the Acts!

Bible: ignorance of

An RE teacher asked a pupil, 'Who knocked down the walls of Jericho?'

'I didn't, Sir; I was away last week.'

So the teacher went to the headmaster. 'Who knocked down the walls of Jericho?' he asked.

'I'm not sure,' said the headmaster. 'I'll come back to you on that one.'

The headmaster wrote to the Minister of Education, 'Who knocked down the walls of Jericho?' he asked.

Eventually he received the reply, 'You just get the wall rebuilt and we'll see that someone pays the bill.'

Books

If he shall not lose his reward who gives a cup of cold water to his thirsty neighbour, what will not be the reward of those who by putting good books into the hands of those neighbours give to them the fountains of eternal life? (Thomas à Kempis)

Brevity

A large dinner party was organised to pay homage to a distinguished man. He spoke to the host beforehand and asked whether, in response to the eulogy, he wanted him to give his short speech or his long speech. The host, not surprisingly, asked for the short speech.

At the close of the dinner and after all the words of praise, the guest stood up and said, 'Thank you!'

The host approached him afterwards and asked him what his long speech would have been. 'Thank you very much!' he replied.

Brevity of life

A notice from the obituary column:

DIED: Salvador Sanchez, 23, World Boxing Council featherweight champion and one of the sport's best fighters; of injuries after his Porsche 928 collided with two trucks, just north of Queretaro, Mexico. A school dropout at 16, Sanchez once explained, 'I found out that I liked hitting people, and I didn't like school, so I started boxing.' A peppery tactician, he wore opponents down for late-round knockouts. His record: 43-1-1.

'I'd like to step down undefeated,' he said last month. 'I'm only 23 and I have all the time in the world.'

*I take it, brother, you've always carried your
Bible under your left arm?*

Busyness

Busyness rapes relationships. It substitutes shallow frenzy for deep friendships. It promises satisfying dreams but delivers hollow nightmares. It feeds the ego but starves the inner man. It fills a calendar or diary but fractures a family. It cultivates a programme but plows under priorities. (Charles Swindoll, *Killing Giants, Pulling Thorns*)

Calling

Memorandum

TO: Jesus, son of Joseph, woodcrafter, Carpenter's Shop, Nazareth.

FROM: Jordan Management Consultants, Jerusalem.

Dear Sir

Thank you for submitting the résumés of the twelve men you have picked for management positions in your new organisation. All of them have now taken our battery of tests; we have not only run the results through our computer, but also arranged personal interviews for each of them with our psychologist and vocational aptitude consultant.

It is the staff opinion that most of your nominees

are lacking in background, education and vocational aptitude for the type of enterprise you are undertaking. They do not have the team concept. We would recommend that you continue your search for persons of experience in managerial ability and proven capability.

Simon Peter is emotionally unstable and given to fits of temper.

Andrew has absolutely no qualities of leadership.

The two brothers, *James and John*, the sons of Zebedee, place personal interest above company loyalty.

Thomas demonstrates a questioning attitude that would tend to undermine morale.

We feel it is our duty to tell you that *Matthew* has been blacklisted by the Greater Jerusalem Better Business Bureau.

James, son of Alphaeus, and *Thaddaeus* definitely have radical leanings, and they both registered a high score on the manic-depressive scale.

One of the candidates, however, shows great potential. He is a man of ability and resourcefulness, meets people well, has a keen business mind and has contacts in high places. He is highly motivated, ambitious and responsible. We recommend *Judas Iscariot* as your controller and right-hand man. All of the other profiles are self-explanatory.

We wish you success in your new venture.

Change

The seven last words of the church: 'We've never done it that way before!'

If the good Lord had wanted us to go metric, he would have had only ten apostles.

Half-way through the church meeting of his tiny Irish congregation, the new minister had a quiet word with the church secretary. 'Do you have a word in Celtic for *mañana*?' he asked.

'Yes,' replied the secretary, 'but it lacks the sense of urgency.'

There are three types of people: those who make things happen; those who watch things happen, and those who haven't a clue what's happening!

Character/Sin

A scorpion, being a poor swimmer, asked a turtle to carry him on his back across a river.

'Are you mad?' exclaimed the turtle. 'You'll sting me while I'm swimming and I'll drown!'

'My dear turtle,' laughed the scorpion, 'if I were to sting you, you would drown and I would go down with you! Now, where is the logic in that?'

'You're right!' cried the turtle. 'Hop on!'

The scorpion climbed aboard and, half-way across the river gave the turtle a mighty sting. As they both sank to the bottom, the turtle resignedly said, 'Do you mind if I ask you something? You said there'd be no logic in your stinging me. Why did you do it?'

'It had nothing to do with logic,' the drowning scorpion replied, sadly. 'It's just my character.'

Character is what you are in the dark. (D L Moody)

Charismatics

How many Charismatics does it take to change a light bulb?

Five: one to change the bulb and four to share the experience.

Church/church growth

In the thrombosis of the church the minister is often the clot.

Those who fail to plan, plan to fail.

Those who aim at nothing are sure to hit it.

A new vicar regularly spent five days of the week in the graveyard, cutting the grass and tidying up. The church council eventually questioned him about this and he replied, 'As five-sevenths of my income come from the dead, I thought I'd spend five-sevenths of my time with them!'

Growing pains

A man got talking to a new colleague and discovered he had six children.

'I wish *I* had six kids', he said ruefully.

'How many do you have, then?' asked his colleague.

'Twelve!'

A slightly cynical minister, on his first flight in a Jumbo Jet, said that it reminded him of his church: several hundred people sitting back looking bored and a few stewards and crew members rushed off their feet!

> Some go to church to take a walk;
> Some go to church to laugh and talk;
> Some go there to meet a friend;
> Some go there their time to spend;
> Some go there to meet a lover;
> Some go there a fault to cover;
> Some go there for speculation;
> Some go there for observation;
> Some go there to doze and nod;
> The wise go there to worship God.

Have you heard about the man who said he didn't intend to come to church again? He had only been twice. The first time as a baby they had poured cold water over him and the second time they joined him for life to a nagging wife. 'Well, watch out,' said the Vicar, 'the next time you come we may throw dirt in your face!'

Church music

When a man from the country returned from a visit to the city, he told his wife, Mary, that he had gone to church and that the choir had sung an anthem.

Mary asked, 'What's an anthem?'

Her husband replied, 'Well, it's like this. If I said, "Mary, the cows are in the corn", that would be like a hymn. But if I said, "Oh Mary! Mary! Mary! The cows are in the corn, the Jersey cow, the Ayrshire cow, the Muley cow; all the cows, all the cows, the cows, the cows are in the corn, the corn, the corn," then that would be an anthem!' (Anglican Digest)

Commitment

When the famous film director, Franco Zeffirelli, announced that he was planning to film the life of

Christ from birth to resurrection, film stars offered their services and some travelled thousands of miles to location sites in Tunisia and Morocco.

James Mason journeyed from Switzerland to play Joseph of Arimathea. Rod Steiger left California to play Pontius Pilate and Laurence Olivier flew from London to take the role of Nicodemus. Many big stars played in minor roles.

Claudia Cardinale was the most determined of the stars. She persisted in asking the director for a part in the film and when she was told that all that remained was the part of the adulteress whom Christ forgave, she accepted. She flew from her home in Rome to Tunisia, arrived on the set on a very hot day, put on her make-up and her costume and spent five hours in the blistering heat before the cameras. The sum total of her speaking part was only three lines.

She was willing to pay a high price in terms of personal discomfort and sacrifice in order to say a few words in a film about Jesus. (Doug Barnett)

Communication breakdown

One of the early Anglican charismatics, Michael Harper, was introduced on American TV as 'the angelican leader of the cosmetic revival'!

I'm so terribly sorry but we've had nothing but problems since we installed a computer!!

And God said to Noah: 'Will you build me an Ark?'

'Yes, Lord. You know that I will. But there's just one question, Lord.'

'Ycs, Noah?'

'What's an Ark?'

Signing the register at a wedding, the best man had difficulty in making his ball-point pen work. 'Put your weight on it,' said the vicar. He duly signed: 'John Smith (ten stone, four pounds).'

A man went round to the tradesman's entrance of a big house and asked if they had any odd jobs that he could do. After a moment's thought the owner said he would pay him £25 to go round to the front of the house and paint the porch.

After only a couple of hours the man came back with the pot of white paint and declared that he had finished the job.

'That was very quick!' exclaimed the owner.

'Yes, well it's not all that big – and, by the way, it's a Mercedes, not a Porsche!'

Six-year old Margaret asked her father when their new baby would talk. He told her that it would not be for two years, since little babies don't talk.

'Oh yes they do!' Margaret insisted. 'Even in the Bible they do!'

'What makes you say that?' he asked.

'When the lady read the Bible this morning in church, she definitely said that Job cursed the day he was born!'

Conformity

He who marries the spirit of the age is sure to be a widower in the next. (G K Chesterton)

We forfeit three-fourths of ourselves in order to be like other people. (Schopenhauer)

Conversion

Ten reasons why I never wash

1 I was made to wash as a child.
2 People who wash are hypocrites – they reckon they're cleaner than other people.
3 There are so many different kinds of soap, I could never decide which one was right.
4 I used to wash, but it got boring, so I stopped.
5 I still wash on special occasions, like Christmas and Easter.
6 None of my friends wash.
7 I'm still young. When I'm older and have got a bit dirtier I might start washing.
8 I really don't have time.
9 The bathroom's never warm enough.
10 People who make soap are only after your money.

Daft, isn't it? We all need to wash, and we know it. There's no argument!

And we all need a personal friendship with Jesus, too. The need may not be quite so obvious, but it's there all the same.

Jesus can do something soap and water can never do: he can make us clean *on the inside*! And that can't be bad!

Like to know how he does it? We'd be glad to explain – without any flannel or soft soap! (Christian Publicity Organisation, Worthing)

Two caterpillars were sitting on a cabbage leaf, looking up at a beautiful butterfly, and one said to the other, 'You'll never get me up in one of those things!'

Revolution transforms everything except the human heart. (Victor Hugo)

Why Communism failed: Communism decrees, 'On every man a new suit.' Christianity says, 'In every suit a new man.'

Covering your tracks

A minister wrote: 'Don't be surprised if you find mistakes in this church newsletter. We print something for everyone. And some people are always looking for mistakes.'

THE ARCHDEACON IS AT 500 YARDS AND CLOSING

The Cross

Our hope lies not in the man we put on the moon, but in the man we put on the cross. (Don Basham)

Death

My grandfather would look through the obituary columns and say to me, 'Strange, isn't it, how everybody seems to die in alphabetical order?'

'I'm not afraid to die; I just don't want to be there when it happens.' (Woody Allen)

Denominations

For Baptists, 'the priesthood of all believers' means that even the Pope is sometimes right.

A man ran to stop another man from flinging himself off a bridge into a river.

'Why are you killing yourself?' he asked.

'I've nothing to live for!'

'Don't you believe in God?'

'Yes, I do.'

'What a coincidence – so do I! Are you a Jew or a Christian?'

'A Christian.'

'What a coincidence – so am I! Protestant or Catholic?'

'Protestant.'

'What a coincidence – so am I! Anglican or Baptist?'

'Baptist.'

'What a coincidence – so am I! Strict and Particular, or General?'

'Strict and Particular.'

'What a coincidence – so am I! Premillennial or Amillennial?'

'Premillennial.'

'What a coincidence – so am I! Partial rapture or Full rapture?'

'Partial rapture.'

At this, the first man sprang on the second and pushed him into the river, shouting 'Die, infidel!'

There was once a preacher, a Baptist and a staunch Baptist at that. No other denomination was really *Christian* in his view. If you weren't a Baptist –

well, you were just the pits! He went to preach at a church that was preparing to take part in a week of prayer for Christian unity. At the end of the meeting he asked,

'How many people in this church are Baptist?'

It was a Baptist church and, knowing his reputation, almost all the local non-Baptists had stayed away. So nearly everyone in the congregation put up their hands – all except one little old lady.

The preacher decided to embarrass her. He told the others to put their hands down and he said to her,

'What denomination are you?'

'I'm a Methodist,' she replied.

'A *what*?'

'A Methodist,' she said.

'And *why* are you a Methodist?' he asked.

'Well,' she said, 'my father was a Methodist and my grandfather was a Methodist, so I'm a Methodist.'

The preacher decided that he would really make his point here, so he said,

'That's simply ridiculous! Suppose your father was a moron and your grandfather was a moron, what would *that* make you?'

The little old lady thought for a moment, then replied,

'I guess that would make me a Baptist!'

You serve God in your way, and we serve him in his.

A Presbyterian, a Methodist and a Baptist were discussing which church Jesus would join if he were to return to earth.

'He would obviously join the Presbyterians,' said the Presbyterian, 'because we have the form of government nearest to the New Testament pattern.'

'No,' said the Methodist, 'he would join *us* because of our emphasis on preaching and fellowship.'

Eventually, they turned to the Baptist, who had been silent all this time. 'And what do you think?' they asked.

He replied, 'I don't see why he should want to transfer his membership!'

Depression

> You can run from war,
> You can run from the law,
> You can run from the cop on the beat.
> You can run from danger,
> You can run from a stranger,
> But you can't run away from your feet.

He was so low he could sit on a cigarette paper and dangle his legs.

VACANCIES

VACANT SEES

Diplomacy

. . . the art of letting someone else have your way.

Disappointment

On his first parachute jump the soldier receives instructions from his sergeant: 'You count to ten and then pull this cord. If the parachute fails you pull the emergency parachute cord here. And then try to land near the lorry down there – they will have a nice cup of tea waiting for you.'

The parachutist counts to ten and pulls the cord. Nothing happens. He pulls the emergency cord. Nothing happens. As he hurtles towards the lorry he is heard to mutter, 'I bet there's no cup of tea, either!'

Discretion

. . . is raising one's eyebrows instead of the roof.

Doublespeak

Dialogue at a dinner party full of showbiz person-
alities:
   'And what are you doing at the moment?'
   'I'm writing a book.'
   'Neither am I . . . '

Evangelism

> When I enter that beautiful city,
> and the saints all around me appear,
> I hope that someone will tell me
> It was *you* who invited me here.

Going to Extremes

A man fell asleep in his usual place in a commuter
train. Somewhat unusually, the train stopped just
short of the station, waiting for the signal to change.
The man woke up with a start, sprang up, opened
the carriage door, stepped out and fell onto the
track. But he quickly climbed back in again. As he
shut the door, he said to his fellow passengers, 'I
bet you think I'm really stupid!'

   Then he walked across to the other door, opened
it, and fell out onto the embankment.

Facts

Facts do not cease to exist because they are ignored!
(Aldous Huxley)

Faith

. . . is trying to believe what you know isn't true.

. . . is sitting on a branch while the Devil is sawing
through it, and believing the tree will fall down!

. . . and its opposite: stupidity

Two friends were looking through a holiday bro-
chure and decided to go on this incredibly cheap
trip to the Carribbean. When the trip got underway
they weren't too surprised to find that the plane
had very few modern amenities (it had only an
outside loo), but they were more surprised when,

somewhere over the Atlantic, the floor opened and they were dropped thousands of feet into the ocean. However, a life-raft was dropped down after them.

As they clambered in, one of them said to the other, 'I suppose they *will* send help for us?'

The other replied, 'Well, they didn't last year!'

Fanaticism

A fanatic is someone who can't change his mind and won't change the subject. (Winston Churchill)

God finds it easier to cool down a fanatic than to warm up a corpse. (George Verwer)

Fighting back

A church near the flight path of London Airport displays a cartoon of Concorde flying past its steeple, with the air hostess telling the pilot, 'The passengers are complaining about the noise of the singing, sir!'

THE NEW READER'S DIGEST BIBLE

DOUBLE GLAZING

FREE SPANNERS OFFER

CUT PRICE PEW WARMERS

Follow-up

An evangelist and a pastor took a holiday together
to go bear hunting in Canada. One evening the
pastor was sitting in their log cabin when he heard
cries for help. Looking out of the window he saw
the evangelist rushing towards the hut, hotly pur-
sued by a huge grizzly bear. The pastor jumped up
to open the door to let his friend in but, at the last
minute, the evangelist side-stepped the door while
the grizzly bear plunged on in. As the evangelist
pulled the door shut from the outside, he yelled,
'You deal with that one – I'll go and get some
more!'

Forgiveness

An Episcopal Church in the United States adver-
tised what it had to offer: 'In the church started
by a man with six wives, forgiveness goes without
saying.'

Every saint has a past and every sinner has a future.
(Oscar Wilde)

When the Devil reminds you of your past, you remind him of his future!

One of the classic films of 1987 was *The Mission*. In it, a soldier, Captain Mendoza, kills his brother in a feud over a woman they both love. Afterwards, desperately depressed and consumed by remorse, he feels that the only way to get rid of his burden of guilt and sin is to perform some sort of penance. So he ties a huge net to his back, fills it with boulders, and sets himself to climb a high mountain.

In the company of a priest and some others, he travels over bracken, gorse and rocks, across rivers and through forests. You see him, cut, bruised and bleeding, a broken figure, crawling up the mountainside, the huge weight dragging behind him. From time to time, the others in the group urge him to let go of the burden. 'You don't have to carry it any more,' they say. But he cannot leave it.

Eventually, reaching the top of the mountain, he collapses, exhausted. And then a little boy comes up to him – and cuts the net from him. As the net and rocks cascade down the mountainside Mendoza is filled with a feeling of total release; his burden is gone and he knows he has been forgiven.

We will not accept into our membership anyone unless he is an active, disciplined, working member in one of our organisations. (Lenin)

Genius

In the Republic of Mediocrity, genius is dangerous. (Robert Ingersoll)

Genius is the ability to reduce the complicated to the simple.

True genius resides in the capacity for evaluation of uncertain, hazardous and conflicting information. (Winston Churchill)

Paderewski, the Polish pianist, was once approached by a woman after one of his concerts. 'Paderewski,' she said, 'you are a genius!'

'Yes, madam,' he replied, 'but for many years before that, I was a drudge.'

The Grand Highway?

Sound theology

Beware: lively worship

Avoid PCCs

Beware: long sermons

 Prone to heresy

 Roof repairs in progress

 Average age of congregation

 Adult baptism practiced

Organ requires tuning

Disagreement among members

Real camel in nativity plays

Whole families baptised
(St John's Bitton, North Yorkshire)

Gratitude

In Ogden Nash's poem, *The Outcome of Mr MacLeod's Gratitude*, he tells of a wife who was always complaining and a husband who managed to be grateful for everything. The last stanza runs:

So she tired of her husband's cheery note
And she stuffed a tea-tray down his throat.
He remarked from the floor, where they found
  him reclining,
'I'm just a MacLeod with a silver lining!'

Gratitude?

A farmer was showing a man round his farm one day when they came to the pig sty – and there was a magnificent pig with a wooden leg. Not surprisingly, the visitor asked about the wooden leg.

The farmer replied, 'Arr . . . now that's a very special pig. One night when we were all in bed, the farm caught fire. But that pig saw it, broke out of the sty, called the fire brigade, threw buckets of water on the fire, then rushed into the farmhouse and rescued me, my wife and the children. Yes, that's a very special pig!'

'And did he lose his leg trying to fight the fire?' enquired the visitor.

'Oh, no! But a very special pig like that – you don't eat it all at once!'

Guidance

Woman to man digging a hole in the road: 'How do you get to the Royal Albert Hall?'
   'Lady, you have to practice!'

Policeman to driver going the wrong way up a one-way street: 'Didn't you see the arrows?'
Driver: 'I didn't even see the Indians!'

Guilt

Man is the only animal who blushes – or needs to!
(Mark Twain)

I'm afraid he's going to want to see more than just your baptism certificate and a video of your wedding!

Healing

An advertisement in the *Southport Visitor* read:
'A healing session by John Cain (of Birkenhead): Owing to illness: meeting cancelled.' (Peterborough, *Daily Telegraph*)

Heaven

In our present condition the joys of heaven would be an acquired taste. (C S Lewis)

Heaven is not just 'pie in the sky by and by'; it's 'steak on the plate while you wait'!

Humility

The *Church Times* recalls a story about the late Dr Newport White when he was Regius Professor of Divinity at Dublin. On one great occasion somebody noticed him sitting unrobed in a pew and whispered, 'Shouldn't you be in the procession?' To which the worthy Doctor replied, 'Just a little ostentatious humility.'

Immaturity

Out of the mouths of babes comes a lot of what they should have swallowed. (Franklin B Jones)

Inconsistency / ups and downs

A parachutist hurtles towards the ground, his parachute having failed to open. As he fumbles and panics he is amazed to pass a man going up.

'Do you know anything about parachutes?' he shouts to him.

'No! Do you know anything about gas ovens?'

The Inner city

A little boy was saying his prayers on the last night before his family moved from Devon: 'Well, it's "goodbye" from me, now, God – we're going to live in London.'

Insincerity

He had a permanent SWEG – a Slimy Wet Evangelical Grin.

He was an Evangellyfish – he stung you with a gospel text and moved off smartly.

Interlude

. . . to wake up the congregation.

I've had a wonderful evening – but this wasn't it. (Groucho Marx)

Life and the Spirit

The neatest, tidiest and most orderly place in town is usually the cemetery!

Uncouth life is better than aesthetic death.

Someone once asked Dwight Moody, the nineteenth-century American evangelist, 'Have you been filled with the Holy Spirit?'
　'Yes,' he replied, 'but I leak!'

Love

> To live above with saints we love,
> Oh! That will be glory!
> To live below with saints we know,
> Well, that's a different story!

Marriage

It is high time that our so-called experts on marriage, the family and the home, turned to the Bible. We have read newspaper columns and listened to counsellors on the radio and TV; psychiatrists have had a land-office business. In it all, the One who performed the first marriage in the Garden of Eden and instituted the union between man and wife has been left out. (Billy Graham)

The greatest thing a man can do for his children is to love their mother. (Michael Cassidy)

Marriage: it starts when you sink into his arms and ends with your arms in his sink.

The average wife would rather have beauty than brains, because she knows that the average husband can see better than he can think.

*Rosey!! I've told you **never** phone me at work!!!*

To keep your marriage brimming
With love in the loving cup,
If ever you're wrong, admit it,
If ever you're right, shut up.
                              (Ogden Nash)

Where the warfare is the hottest
In the battlefields of life,
You'll find the Christian soldier
Represented by his wife.

A silly and childish game is one at which your wife
can beat you.

My wife and I were very happy for thirty years –
and then we met!

I love the human race. All of my family belong to it, and some of my husband's family, too.

Marriage is a woman's way of calling a meeting to order.

Materialism

Let's stop loving things and using people, and start using things and loving people.

Meaning of life

Mark Twain, whose literature has been enjoyed by many, became morose and weary of life. Shortly before his death, he wrote: 'A myriad of men are born; they labour and sweat and struggle . . . they squabble and scold and fight; they scramble for little mean advantages over each other; age creeps upon them; infirmities follow . . . those they love are taken from them, and the joy of life is turned to aching grief. It [release] comes at last – the only unpoisoned gift earth had ever had for them – and they vanish from a world where they were of no consequence . . . a world which will lament them a day and forget them forever.'

Meekness

Seen on a church noticeboard: 'The meek will inherit the earth – if that's all right with you.'

Modesty

Church member to vicar after the service: 'You were really good this morning!'

Modestly, the vicar replies, 'Oh, it wasn't me; it was the Lord.'

Church member: 'You weren't that good!'

Money

From a church bulletin: 'A number of buttons have been found among the coins in recent collections. In future, please rend your hearts and not your garments.'

As the parishioners were leaving church after a service, one woman said, in a loud voice, 'I've nothing but praise for the new vicar!' A rather glum old sidesman who was passing overheard her and remarked, 'So I noticed when I passed you the collection bag.'

Musical misquotes

'I will make you vicious old men . . . '

'Grind us together, Lord . . . '

'Who is a gardening pod like thee?'

A little girl had a teddybear with a lazy eye. She called it 'Gladly', because she had sung about it in church: 'Gladly, my cross-eyed bear . . . '

Obedience

A group of American tourists were on a conducted tour of the House of Commons when a Labour Lord entered the central lobby, wearing his ceremonial garb. He wanted to catch the attention of Neil Kinnock, who was over on the far side of the House, so he shouted, 'Neil!' And fifty Americans dutifully knelt.

Optimism/pessimism

'Twixt optimist and pessimist
The difference is droll:
The optimist sees the doughnut,
The pessimist sees the hole.

An optimist? The woman who slips her feet back into her shoes when the preacher says, 'And finally . . .'

Just because you occasionally feel fed up, don't despair! Remember that the sun has a 'sinking spell' every night but rises again in the morning.

Originality

There is no such thing as an original joke.
(Stephen Gaukroger and Nick Mercer)

I fear I have nothing original in me – excepting original sin. (Thomas Campbell)

Originality is the art of concealing your source. (Franklin Jones)

The Pastor

Pastor, Priest, Vicar, Minister and friend . . .

whatever we call him or her, it's still a tough job:

If he visits his flock, he's nosey.
If he doesn't, he's a snob.
If he preaches longer than ten minutes, it's too
long.
If he preaches less than ten minutes, he can't have
prepared his sermon.
If he runs a car, he's worldly.
If he doesn't, he's always late for appointments.
If he tells a joke, he's flippant.
If he doesn't, he's far too serious.
If he starts the service on time, his watch must be
fast.
If he's a minute late, he's keeping the congregation
waiting.
If he takes a holiday, he's never in the parish.
If he doesn't, he's a stick-in-the-mud.
If he runs a gala or bazaar, he's money mad.
If he doesn't, there's no social life in the parish.
If he has the Church painted and redecorated, he's
extravagant.
If he doesn't, the Church is shabby.
If he's young, he's inexperienced.
If he's getting old, he ought to retire.
But . . .
When he dies, there's never been anyone like him!
(Adapted from *Beda Review*, via *Catholic Herald*)

According to a writer in *Parson and Parish*, when churches seek a new incumbent they expect, 'the strength of an eagle, the grace of a swan, the gentleness of a dove, the friendliness of a sparrow and the night hours of an owl . . . Then when they catch the bird, they expect him to live on the food of a canary.'

The Deacon's prayer: 'Lord, send us a poor, humble minister. You keep him humble and we'll keep him poor.'

'What's a Deacon, Johnny?'

'You put it on a hill and when the enemy comes you set fire to it!'

. . . It's going to be one of those days . . .

Pastor and Doctor

Mrs Huff is up the miff tree
On a scat fixed good and firm;
And she'd like to tell the pastor
A few things to make him squirm.

Mrs Huff was sick abed, sir,
Yes, sir, sick abed a week!
And the pastor didn't call, sir,
Never even took a peek.

When I asked her if the doctor
Called to see her, she said, 'Sure!'
And she looked as if she thought I
Needed some good mental cure.

Then I asked her how the doctor
Knew that sickness laid her low,
And she said that she had called him
On the 'phone and told him so.

Now the doctor gets his bill paid
With a nicely written cheque;
But the pastor, for not knowing,
Simply gets it in the neck.

How many pastors does it take to change a light bulb?

Only one – but the bulb has really got to want to change.

Two Yorkshire farmers were discussing their respective clerics. One said: 'Our fellow's got foot and mouth disease. 'E don't visit and 'e can't preach!'

A minister's job is to comfort the afflicted and to afflict the comfortable!

A new shorthand code for churches trying to decide what sort of minister they are looking for:

A YUMMY: A young upwardly mobile minister.

A MUMMY: A middle-aged upwardly mobile minister.

A GUMMY: A geriatric upwardly mobile minister.

Persistence

I've been knocked down, kicked around,
Some people scandalise my name,
But here I am, talking about Jesus just the same.
I've been knocked down, kicked around,
But like a moth drawn to the flame,
Here I am, talking about Jesus just the same.

(Larry Norman)

If you're ever tempted to give up, just think of Brahms. He took seven years to compose his famous lullaby – he kept falling asleep at the piano! (Robert Orben)

By perseverence the snail reached the Ark. (Spurgeon)

Consider the postage stamp: its usefulness consists in the ability to stick to one thing until it gets there. (Josh Billings)

Seen on the side of an ice-cream van: 'Often licked but never beaten!'

Frogs in cream

Two frogs fell into a can of cream,
Or so I've heard it told;
The sides of the can were shiny and steep,
The cream was deep and cold.

'Oh, what's the use?' croaked Number 1,
'Tis fate; no help's around.
Goodbye, my friends! Goodbye, sad world!'
And, weeping still, he drowned.

But Number 2, of sterner stuff,
Dog-paddled in surprise,
The while he wiped his creamy face
And dried his creamy eyes.

'I'll swim awhile, at least,' he said,
Or so I've heard he said;
'It really wouldn't help the world
If one more frog were dead.'

An hour or two he kicked and swam,
Not once he stopped to mutter;
But kicked and kicked and swam and kicked,
then hopped out, via butter!

(T C Hamlet)

*I was leading 'choruses with actions', if you
must know!*

The Personal touch

Here is a love story. A young man and a young woman were deeply in love and, while he was away with the Navy for three years, he wrote to her every day, without fail. At the end of the three years came the happy wedding – she married the postman.

Potential

One can count the number of seeds in an apple, but one cannot count the number of apples in a seed. (Llandridod Wells Church magazine)

Praise

The most obvious fact about praise – whether of God or anything – strangely escaped me . . . I had not noticed how the humblest, and at the same time most balanced and capacious minds, praised most, while the cranks, misfits and malcontents praised least. The good critics found something to praise in many imperfect works; the bad ones continually narrowed down the list . . . The healthy and un-affected man, even if luxuriously brought up and widely experienced in good cookery, could praise a very modest meal . . . the snob found fault with all . . . Praise almost seems to be inner health made audible. (C S Lewis)

Prayer

A mother overheard her young son praying one day: ' . . . and if you give me a bike, Lord, then I'll be good for a whole week.'

She interrupted him and said, 'Now, Johnny, it's no good trying to bargain with God. He won't answer prayers like that!'

A few days later she overheard him praying again: ' . . . and if you give me a new bike, Lord, I'll be good for *three* weeks!'

'Johnny,' said his mother gently, 'I thought I told you it was no good trying to strike bargains with the Lord. He doesn't respond to that sort of prayer.'

A few days later the mother was cleaning the house and, to her amazement, found right at the bottom of the airing cupboard, a little statue of the madonna that had stood on the sideboard. She guessed that this must be something to do with Johnny and went up to his room to find him. He wasn't there but on the window sill she found a note which read: 'OK, Lord, if you ever want to see your mother again . . . !'

Heard at the prayer meeting: 'Lord, it was such a fantastic meeting last Saturday! All the things that happened and the "words" we got . . . You should've been there, Lord!'

The nineteenth-century Baptist preacher, Charles Spurgeon, was once asked, 'When should I pray? Should I pray when I don't feel like it?'

He replied, 'Pray when you feel like it, because God will bless you; pray when you don't feel like it, because that is when you need it most.'

You probably remember playing with iron filings at school. You run a magnet over a bunch of iron filings and they all stand to attention, or move to the right or to the left. Long before the magnet makes physical contact with the filings, something is happening. Why? Because an invisible power, magnetism, is affecting them.

In the same way, prayer, which is invisible and spiritual, affects that which is visible and physical.

Preaching / Reconciliation

Bishop Festo Kivengere told the story of how he was going off to preach after a row with his wife. The Holy Spirit said to him, 'Go back and pray with your wife!'

He argued, 'I'm due to preach in twenty minutes. I'll do it afterwards.'

'OK,' said the Holy Spirit. 'You go and preach; I'll stay with your wife.'

Preaching (bad preaching)

'My lips are hermeneutically sealed.'

Well, the minister got to know a *little* Greek and Hebrew while he was at College. The Greek ran the kebab shop and the Hebrew made his suits!

His preaching cost nothing – and it was worth it! (Mark Twain)

For goodness' sake, George! You're on holiday!

Little girl to mummy: 'Mummy, why does the pastor pray before his sermon?'

She replied, 'He's asking God to help him preach a good sermon.'

'Mummy, why doesn't God answer his prayer?'

Prepared?

The 'kairos' moment

An unemployed actor finally landed a one-line part in a big West End play. He only had five words to say: 'Hark! How the cannons roar!' and spent all his time practicing different ways of saying it.

On the morning of the first day of the performance he ate his breakfast, muttering, 'Hark! How the cannons roar!' As he caught the tube into the city he repeated to himself, 'Hark! How the cannons roar!' Finally, as he stood in the wings waiting for his moment to come, he said over and over, 'Hark! How the cannons roar!'

At last the moment came. He walked on stage and his cue came, 'Bang!'

'What was that!?' he cried.

Principles

When a man approves of something in principle it means he hasn't the slightest intention of putting it into practice. (Bismarck)

A snippet in a national paper read: 'A trustee of the British Vegetarian Society and a member of its National Council, has resigned after he was found selling beefburgers at his village store at Tollerton near York.'

A case of principles suspended for personal financial reasons?

Procrastination

The Devil doesn't care how much good we do, as long as we don't do it today.

Procrastination is my sin,
It brings me naught but sorrow.
I know that I should stop it,
In fact, I will – tomorrow!

(Gloria Pitzer)

Why put off till tomorrow what you can safely put off till the week after next?

Prophecy (false)

'Thus says the Lord: I have nothing against you . . . as far as I know . . . '

Rebellion

A father repeatedly told his little boy to sit down on the back seat of the car. He remained standing until eventually, exasperated, the father physically sat the boy down.

The little boy grimaced and muttered, 'I may be sitting down on the outside, but I'm standing up on the inside!'

Repentance

A painter not particularly noted for his honesty decided to water down the paint but charge his customer for the full amount he should have used. Unfortunately for him, he carried the process rather too far with the result that the finished work looked so bad that even the most short-sighted client would notice it.

'What can I do now?' he wailed.

From the heavens a great voice boomed, 'Repaint! And thin no more!'

A new Christian wrote to the Inland Revenue: 'I can't sleep at night, so I am enclosing £100 I forgot to declare.

PS. If I still can't sleep, I will send the rest.'

Sleep with clean hands, either kept clean all day by integrity or washed clean at night by repentance. (John Donne)

It was bank holiday weekend and a long queue had formed at the petrol station. When at last it was the vicar's turn, the attendant apologised for the long delay: 'They knew they were going to make this trip, yet they all waited until the last minute to get ready!'

The vicar smiled ruefully. 'I know what you mean', he said. 'It's like that in my business, too!'

Doctor to overweight patient: 'Here's a list of what you must eat: lettuce, carrots, cabbage . . . '

'That's fine, doctor', interrupted the patient, 'but do I take them before or after meals?'

Responsibility

Young boy to his father, who is reading his appalling end-of-term report: 'What do you think the trouble is, Dad? Heredity or environment?'

Restoration

In the former home of Sir Winston Churchill there
is a large model of a ship. It is made out of thousands of discarded, burnt-out matches. All those
finished, useless items have been patiently moulded
together and re-formed into something amazingly
beautiful.

That's precisely what God wants to do with us.
He wants to take the blackened embers of ruined
lives, with all their failures and sin, and to create
something beautiful and special for himself out of
them. What seems bankrupt and useless to us is,
to God, material to take up and turn into something
special and glorious.

Risk-taking

God equipped us with necks – we should occasionally stick them out!

If you don't go overboard, you tend not to make a
splash.

Salvation

The Pit

A man fell into a pit and couldn't get himself out.

A *subjective* person came along and said, 'I feel for you down there.'

An *objective* person came along and said, 'It's logical that someone would fall down there.'

A *Pharisee* said, 'Only bad people fall into pits.'

A *news reporter* wanted the exclusive story on the man's pit.

Confucius said, 'If you had listened to me, you wouldn't be in that pit.'

Buddha said, 'Your pit is only a state of mind.'

A *realist* said, 'That's a PIT.'

A *scientist* calculated the pressure necessary (PSI) to get him out of the pit.

A *geologist* told him to appreciate the rock strata in the pit.

A *tax man* asked if he was paying taxes on the pit.

The council inspector asked if he had a permit to dig a pit.

An *evasive* person came along and avoided the subject of his pit altogether.

A *self-pitying* person said, 'You haven't seen anything until you've seen MY pit!'

A *charismatic* said, 'Just confess that you're not in a pit.'

An *optimist* said, 'Things could be worse.'
A *pessimist* said, 'Things will get worse.'

Jesus, seeing the man, took him by the hand and lifted him out of the pit. (Kenneth D Filkins)

Salvation is moving from living death to deathless life. (Jack Odell)

Self sacrifice

The trouble with a living sacrifice is that it keeps crawling off the altar!

He is no fool who gives up what he cannot keep to gain what he can never lose. (Jim Elliot)

Sermons

Several years ago the *British Weekly* printed a letter to the editor:
'Dear Sir,
I notice that ministers seem to set a great deal of

importance on their sermons and spend a great deal of time in preparing them. I have been attending services quite regularly for the past thirty years and during that time, if I estimate correctly, I have listened to no less than three thousand sermons. But, to my consternation, I discover I cannot remember a single one of them. I wonder if a minister's time might be more profitably spent on something else?

Yours sincerely . . . '

That letter triggered an avalanche of angry responses for weeks. Sermons were castigated and defended by lay people and clergy, but eventually a single letter closed the debate:

'Dear Sir,

I have been married for thirty years. During that time I have eaten 32,000 meals – mostly of my wife's cooking. Suddenly, I have discovered that I cannot remember the menu of a single meal. And yet, I received nourishment from every one of them. I have the distinct impression that without them I would have starved to death long ago.

Yours sincerely . . . '

(James Berkley)

A sermon doesn't have to be eternal to be immortal.

*Good morning – I have a sermon-a-gram
for you!!*

A little boy in church asked his father, as the offering bags came round, 'Daddy, what does that mean?'

'They're collecting our money for God.'

As they knelt for prayer, the little boy asked, 'Daddy, what does that mean?'

'It means we're talking to God.'

And when the minister removed his watch at the start of the sermon, laying it in front of him on the pulpit, the little boy asked, 'Daddy, what does that mean?'

'Absolutely nothing!'

'I don't mind people looking at their watches while I'm preaching, but I get worried when they take them off and shake them!'

'I don't mind people looking at their watches when I preach, but it worries me when they get out their diaries.'

One Sunday morning, the vicar apologised to his congregation for the sticking-plaster on his face. 'I was thinking about my sermon and cut my face,' he said.

Afterwards, in the collection plate he found a note that read, 'Next time, why not think about your face and cut the sermon?'

A good sermon leaves you wondering how the preacher knew so much about you.

A vicar about to speak at a formal dinner was announced by the MC with the words, 'Pray for the silence of the Reverend Smith.'

Service

All the holy men seem to have gone off and died. There's no one left but us sinners to carry on the ministry. (Jamie Buckingham)

I take comfort from the fact that it was willing amateurs who built the Ark, whereas professionals built the Titanic.

Sin

On the church notice board was a poster which read: 'Are you tired of sin? Then come inside.'

Underneath someone had added, 'If not, phone Bayswater 23769.'

Sin: putting worst things first. (Joseph Gancher)

I'm more afraid of my own heart than of the Pope and all his cardinals! (Martin Luther)

You cannot play with sin and overcome it at the same time. (J C Macaulay)

Sin's consequences

Most of us spend the first six days of each week sowing wild oats and the seventh praying for a crop failure.

Sloth

Two men were walking along when one suddenly turned and stamped viciously on a snail.
  'What did you do that for?' asked the other.
  'Oh, it's been following me around all day!'

I see covetousness has risen to number three!

Spiritual warfare

The *Encylopaedia Britannica* describes Joseph Lister, the nineteenth-century medic, as 'the father of antiseptic surgery'. During the course of his work Lister was disturbed by the high proportion of patients who died after operations, not because of any problem with the operations themselves, but from post-operative infections.

He became convinced that infinitesimal microbes, invisible to the naked eye, were causing the infections. So he began to develop a number of antiseptic solutions with which to treat the wounds. Sure enough, the proportion of patients dying from infections decreased.

In the same way, there are evil spiritual forces at work in our world today. They cannot be seen, but they wreak havoc in people's lives, causing them to fall into temptation, moving evil men into positions of national power, manipulating people's emotions, tearing them apart and destroying them.

But just as Lister's contemporaries dismissed his theory of destructive microbes, many Christians today are ignorant or dismissive of spiritual realities. Yet we have the powerful spiritual 'antiseptic' of prayer to use against them and it is vital that we learn to do so.

Standing up for the faith

A police sergeant with a class of cadets asked, 'Imagine you're on duty when two cars smash into each other. You are just about to go to their aid when you notice an articulated lorry heading down the hill towards this blind corner where the accident occurred. You hear a scream and see that the shock of the crash has sent a pregnant woman on the pavement into premature labour. Meanwhile, a fireball from one of the car's petrol tanks is heading towards a crowded pub full of under-age drinkers. What do you do?'

An intelligent young cadet spoke up, 'Slip off my uniform and merge with the crowd, sarge!'

A great oak is only a little nut that held its ground.

Stand-ins

We're so glad you agreed to come today – we asked ten other preachers who said 'no'!

As the substitute preacher stood in the pulpit he noticed a piece of old cardboard filling in the gap in a beautiful, but broken, stained-glass window.

'You know,' he said, 'standing in for such an eminent preacher today, I feel a bit like that cardboard in the stained-glass window – a poor substitute for the real thing.'

After the service, one of the congregation greeted him warmly at the door: 'I want you to know,' he said, 'that you weren't a piece of cardboard this morning – you were a real pane!'

The curate had stepped in to take the sermon at very short notice, because the vicar was ill. At the end of the sermon he explained apologetically, 'At such short notice I'm afraid I just had to rely on the Holy Spirit. Next week I hope to do better!'

Stewardship

The huge, brass offertory plates were passed around the congregation one Sunday evening – and returned almost empty to the vicar. He took them, held them up to heaven and prayed, 'Lord, we thank you for the safe return of these plates . . . '

Tradition

Tradition is the living faith of the dead. Honour it! Traditionalism is the dead faith of the living. Abandon it!

Transformation

The audience was waiting for the brilliant pianist to come out onto the stage. Then, to everyone's embarrassment, a little boy wandered up onto the stage and started banging out one, harsh note on the *Steinway*. Suddenly, the maestro appeared in the wings and made his way over to the boy.

Standing behind him as he banged away tunelessly, he began to weave a melody around the note, taking it up into his larger tune and transforming it into something beautiful. After a few moments, the maestro gently led the boy away from the piano and together they took a bow to the audience's applause. The little boy wandered back to his seat – not embarrassed, not having been made to look foolish.

In the same way, Jesus can take the harsh, discordant, out-of-tune moments of our lives – perhaps a time of sexual sin, or of cowardice or defeat in some other way – and can weave his own purposes around them. As we let him do this, he transforms our mistakes and failures, bringing out of them something he can use for his glory.

Trust

A man fell off a cliff but managed to grab hold of a branch on his way down. He hung there and shouted up to the top, 'Is anybody up there?'

'Yes,' came the reply, 'God is up here!'

'Can you help me, God?'

'Yes.'

'What do you want me to do?'

'Let go of the branch.'

There was a pause.

'Is there anybody else up there?'

*A funny thing happened to me on the way to
the pulpit tonight . . .*

Even if you think you have someone eating out of your hand, it's still advisable to count your fingers afterwards!

There's only one thing better than a friend you can trust, and that's a friend who trusts you.

Truth

Men occasionally stumble over the truth, but most of them pick themselves up and hurry off as if nothing had happened. (Winston Churchill)

Verbosity

In a small trumpet blast against bureaucratic verbosity, this list is circulating around Government departments in Washington:

The Lord's Prayer: 56 words.
The twenty-third Psalm: 118 words.
The Gettysburg address: 226 words.
The ten commandments: 297 words.
The United States Department of Agriculture Order on the price of cabbage: 15,629 words.

Wise living

A pilot came aboard a large tanker to help bring it into harbour. The captain asked him if he really knew where all the rocks were. 'No,' he replied, 'but I know where there aren't any!'

Women

The Baptist church deacons decided to invite their woman minister to go fishing with them. They were fifty yards or so from the shore when she said, apologetically, 'I'm sorry – I've forgotten my fishing rod!'

So she hopped out of the boat, walked across the water to the bank and picked up the rod. As she strolled back one deacon was heard to mutter, 'Typical of a woman – always forgetting things!'

Wonder

The most beautiful and the most profound emotion we can experience is the sensation of the mystical. It is the power of all true science. He to whom this emotion is a stranger, who can no longer wonder, and stand rapt in awe, is as good as dead. (Albert Einstein)

Work

The Pope was asked on one occasion, 'How many people work here at the Vatican?' He replied, 'Oh, about half of them.'

*I sometimes worry that he tries to make
his family services too entertaining!*

Worship

The Danish philosopher, Kierkegaard, compared worship to a dramatic production.

In worship, it often seems as though the worship leader is the actor and God is the prompter, whispering into his ear, telling him what to do next. The congregation listen and, at the end, they 'applaud' if they like the way he's led worship, or throw things if they don't!

But Kierkegaard said that's all back to front. In reality, God is the audience, the congregation are the actors and the person leading worship is the prompter, simply keeping the production going.

So when we come together to worship, we come wanting to please God alone, offering to him our very best.

Seen on a church noticeboard: 'You aren't too bad to come in; you aren't too good to stay out!'

Young people

Some things never change . . .

The children now love luxury; they show disrespect
for elders and love chatter in the place of exercise.
Children are tyrants, not the servants of their
households. They no longer rise when their elders
enter the room. They contradict their parents, chatter before company, gobble up dainties at the table,
cross their legs and tyrannise their teachers.
(Socrates, 469–399 BC)

I see no hope for the future of our people if they
are dependent on the frivolous youth of today, for
certainly all youth are reckless beyond words . . .
When I was young we were taught to be discreet
and respectful of elders, but the present youth are
exceedingly impatient of restraint. (Hesiod, Greek
poet, eighth-century BC)

ZZZZZZZzzz

1001
STUNNING
SERMON
ILLUSTRATIONS